When the Sun Shines on Antarctica

And Other Poems about the Frozen Continent

Irene Latham

illustrated by Anna Wadham

M MILLBROOK PRESS/MINNEAPOLIS

For Papa (Kenneth E. Dykes Sr.), who taught me to love the world—and to write about it —I.L.

For Leo —A.W.

The author would like to thank James McClintock, Endowed University Professor of Polar and Marine Biology at the University of Alabama at Birmingham, for reviewing the text.

Millbrook Press
A division of Lerner Publishing Group, Inc.
241 First Avenue North
Minneapolis, MN 55401 USA

For reading levels and more information, look up this title at www.lernerbooks.com.

Main body text set in Gill Sans Infant Std 15/18. Typeface provided by Monotype Typography.

Library of Congress Cataloging-in-Publication Data

Latham, Irene.
    When the sun shines on Antarctica : and other poems about the frozen continent / by Irene Latham ; illustrated by Anna Wadham.
        pages cm
    ISBN 978-1-4677-5216-9 (lb : alk. paper) — ISBN 978-1-4677-9729-0 (eb pdf)
    1. Natural history—Antarctica—Juvenile literature. 2. Summer—Antarctica—Juvenile literature. I. Wadham, Anna, illustrator. II. Title.
    QH84.2.L38 2016
    508.989—dc23   2015001641

Manufactured in the United States of America
1 – PC – 12/31/15

Contents

When the Sun Shines on Antarctica

Icebergs brighten
as the sky peels

itself of darkness
and stretches awake.

Glaciers murmur.
Penguins reunite

and seals rouse
from slumber.

Whales breach
and blow;

waves rush
and slush

against shifting
ice shelves.

Welcome,
Summer.

We've been waiting
for you.

Positioned at the bottom of the world, Antarctica is the coldest continent. It's basically an island cloaked in ice. Summer lasts from when the sun rises in October to when it sets in March—like one very long day! Temperatures during this time usually stay well below freezing, allowing Antarctica's wildlife to feed and breed. Although the continent has no permanent human residents, each year several thousand scientists travel there to conduct research. Climate change is an important area of study, as rising temperatures cause Antarctica's surface ice to melt. This melting has the potential to affect weather worldwide, to cause flooding along Earth's coastal areas, and to disrupt the entire planet's ecosystem.

Adélie Seeking Adélie

Wanted: a guy with a white-ringed eye
who looks just like me.

An accomplished builder
who borders the nest with the best pebbles

to protect my eggs from the dregs
of melting snow.

A boy with a pleasing bray
who will stay all summer.

A mate who will meet me
             here

year after year
after year.

After months at sea, Adélie penguins return to the Antarctic continent to breed during the summer season. These loud, hyperactive penguins are medium sized and live in large colonies called rookeries. To attract a female, males dig shallow nests with their feet and strategically place stones along the edges to create a rim. The bigger the nest, the more impressed the female. Because nest-building is so competitive and because nests are built within pecking distance of one another, Adélie penguins will often steal stones from their neighbors. Once the female selects a mate, she generally lays two eggs, which increases the chance of at least one egg surviving. Each summer she returns to the nesting site to repeat these courtship and breeding rituals.

A New Coat for Mrs. Weddell

Bored
of her mottled,
spotted fur,

she hauls
herself
onto the ice

to shop
for a fresh
summer style.

Off
comes the heavy,
dingy brown.

In its place,
a sleek coat
grows—

the perfect
match for
her smile.

Named after British Antarctic explorer Sir James Weddell, Weddell seals have small catlike, whiskered faces attached to large, inflated bodies. Summer brings molting season, which is the time when these seals shed their old fur. This makes a mess of the ice shelf, but it keeps the seals cool during the warmer weather and also prepares them for the coming winter season. Weddell seals nap for hours on the ice, their huge bellies soaking up the sun. But don't be fooled by these lazy displays. Underwater, these seals are adept hunters. Not only can they hold their breath for as long as forty-five minutes and descend to depths of up to 2,000 feet (610 meters), these seals also hunt by blowing air bubbles into cracks in the ice to flush out small fish.

Chinstrap Penguin first family portrait

Now that the shell
has been shed,

Mother and Father
marvel over each tuft
of fluff.

Together they guard
against weather and foe—

shoulders cloaked,
bellies disguised as ice,
caps strapped on tight.

Baby comes bundled
in a soft, gray cloud

with oar-shaped wings
that flap without sound,
tiny beak a miracle

peeping
more, more, more.

Chinstrap penguins are identified by the thin line of black feathers that runs along their white cheeks, resembling the strap of a bicycle helmet. Like other Antarctic penguin species, chinstrap penguins share parenting duties. During the summer brooding season, they take turns keeping the egg warm. Once the chick hatches, it is fed regurgitated krill, straight from the parents' mouths. When the chick is hungry, it taps on a parent's beak. As soon as the beak opens, the chick sticks its whole head inside the parent's mouth to feast. This prevents the meal from being stolen by predators or other penguins.

11

Southern Giant Petrel at the Seashore

Petrel
doesn't do
sandcastles
or suntans—
he's more
like a flying
trash can.

His belly
is where all
the garbage
goes;
his beak
is the lid
that never
stays closed.

Careful,
don't come
too near—
or Petrel
will spew
a rotten brew
all over you.

Southern giant petrels may look like oversized seagulls, but they behave more like vultures. A migrating species, they fly in for the summer to cruise the Antarctic shore for dead seals and other animals. When they find a carcass, they often gorge themselves until they become too heavy to fly. When this happens, their only defense when threatened is to vomit the contents of their stomachs, which is an awful-smelling combination of rotten, partially digested flesh and oil. This has earned them the nicknames stinkpot, stinker, and glutton.

Flora in a Frozen Land

I.
Hair grass sprouts
like beach umbrellas,
to shade the piebald rocks—

becomes a cluster
of gossiping girls
sunbathing the day away.

II.
Red algae grows
weary of white,

stains the snow plains
with a checkered spread—

picnics on sunlight.

III.
Moss creeps along
dry valleys—

slowly,
carefully—

unfolds green blankets
soft enough

to swaddle
a newborn seal.

Due to Antarctica's low light, freezing temperatures, poor soil, and lack of rain, plant life (flora) is limited. There are no trees or shrubs. However, many species of moss, lichen, and algae flourish on the continent. Summertime is when the flowers bloom—hair grass and Antarctic pearlwort brighten the stark landscape with bouquets in shades of white, yellow, and green peeking from rocky cracks and crevices. Their populations are increasing, possibly due to rising temperatures associated with climate change.

15

Antarctic Singers in Concert

Humpbacks
claim the stage
with a leap,
breach,

     d
       i
         v
           e.

They grunt
and whistle-chirp,
to begin
their lullaby.

Silverfish
hem their
sun-rippled
gowns.

Barnacles
sparkle
as the notes
float down.

Listen for
that moment
when their voices
pause,

and you
will hear
the ocean's
applause.

Humpback whales are the most common type of baleen whale found in the rich summer Antarctic waters. Each whale pod's unique song contains both high notes and low notes punctuated by rests—just like music created by humans. When humpback whales sing, they hang head down in the water, their flippers gently flapping to help them maintain the position. Whale song is most often heard during breeding season, but scientists suspect this form of communication extends far beyond courtship rituals. Under the right conditions, whale song may travel up to 5 miles (8 kilometers) underwater.

KRILL IN SPACE

The sea
is their universe

as they swim,
sway,
        drift—

a trillion
tiny astronauts

without
a ship.

They weave
through galaxies

of gobbling
nets,

dodge
black holes

that look like safe
caves to explore—

        but aren't.

Krill, which are only the size of a large paper clip, live in the Southern Ocean that surrounds Antarctica. Up close, they look like teeny opaque shrimp. They feast on microscopic phytoplankton. In turn, many species of birds, seals, penguins, and whales feast on krill. This makes krill essential to the Antarctic food chain. Photographs taken by satellites in space show swarms of krill so dense that they look like storm clouds in the water. Experts estimate that the combined mass of all krill is greater than the mass of all the humans on Earth.

Beware the brinicle!

Like a frozen
lightning rod

or a jagged
magic wand,

it daggers
down—

zap—

to cast
an icy spell

on the sea
floor,

entombing
all it touches.

A brinicle is created when salt water drips from summer's melting sea ice and sinks rapidly into Antarctic waters. This sinking brine is so cold that it causes the water around it to instantly freeze. It gets its name from the combination of brine and icicle, and it resembles an icicle hanging from the eaves of a house—until it reaches the sea floor. Then the brinicle fans out, encasing sea stars and whatever other life-forms it encounters, essentially freezing them to death.

BATTLE OF THE BULL ELEPHANT SEALS

Welcome, Ladies and Gentlemen
to the title event of the summer:

Beachmaster of Antarcticaaaaaaa!

At stake, the fate of fifty cows
and the right to roam the beach.

In the white corner, the defending champ:
Bull "the Nose" Elephantinoooooooo

and in the gray, a brave new face:
Elephant Van Zant Sealiooooooooooo!

(Crowd growls, seals ROAR!)

Let the brawl begin!

Southern elephant seals are the largest of all seals. Males can grow to 20 feet (6 m) in length and weigh up to 8,800 pounds (4,000 kilograms). Females are called cows, and they grow to about half the size of the males. Summer marks the breeding season when males gather forty to fifty cows and defend their territories against other males. Fights begin with bellows and blows and can last from a few minutes up to half an hour. Injuries are often minor scratches and bruises, but seals' huge canine teeth can also draw blood and even cause scarring. These wounds are often visible on a male elephant seal's proboscis. This wrinkly flap of skin looks like an elephant's trunk, giving these seals their name.

GENTOO PENGUIN JUMPS IN

After cozy days
in the nest,

after meals delivered
by my parents,

after guarded naps
and hunting lessons,

after shedding fluff
and sprouting new feathers,

after long, sunny days
spent with others my age—

suddenly
   the sea

   doesn't seem
         too vast for me.

         Splash!

Gentoo penguins are easily distinguished from other Antarctic species by their headband of white feathers and their bright orange beaks and feet. As the summer progresses and chicks grow more mature, the parents leave them in créches, which are large groups of juvenile penguins cared for by one or more adults. This separation helps prepare the chicks for life on their own. When the parents return from the sea, they call from a distance and wait for the chicks to locate them. This creates a flurry of hungry juveniles, all competing for food. As soon as the chicks molt and grow their adult waterproof plumage, they are ready to fledge, or leave the rookery. Some gentoo parents still find and feed their fledglings. No other Antarctic penguin species cares so long for its young.

FLiGHT OF THE MiDGE

I have no
wings
to help
me
fly,

so I
leap
to hitch
a ride
on passersby.

I touch
down
on ice and
sometimes
sea,

where I
fight
to get
all six legs
under me.

Then
I skim
the wild,
cresting
waves—

can you
see
I'm just
pretending
to be brave?

Even though the wingless Antarctic midge (Belgica antarctica) measures less than half an inch (1.3 centimeters) in length, it is the largest insect and only true land animal living in Antarctica. The lack of wings helps prevent these insects from being blown away by Antarctica's brutal winds. Midges spend the majority of their two-year lives as larvae. Adults live for just ten days during the summer, long enough for them to mate and for females to lay their eggs. Adaptations for survival include clumping together to prevent water loss and the ability to survive the freezing of bodily fluids.

Emperor Penguins at Play

At the top of the hill
they belly flop,
                     drop,
slide, and glide on built-in sleds.

Out in the ocean,
eager to fly,
they *swim,*   *breathe,*   *swim*
as they leapfrog waves.

In need of rest,
they board an ice ship
where they ride and revive,
play endless rounds
                     of Red Light, Green Light,
                                        Penguin Says,
                                             and I Spy.

As the summer season nears its end, emperor penguin chicks are ready to begin their independent adult lives. The largest of Antarctica's penguins, they can grow to over 3 feet (1 m) tall and weigh up to 80 pounds (36 kg). When they want to go faster on the ice, they toboggan by sliding on their bellies. But underwater is where these penguins really fly. Their average swimming speed is 6 miles (10 km) per hour, which is faster than the fastest human swimmer. To keep their speed when hunting or fleeing predators, they porpoise in and out of the water. What looks like a fun game of hide-and-seek is actually a matter of life or death.

Leopard Seal Spots a Meal

She stalks
with a leopard's stealth.

She too sports whiskers
and a speckled hide.

Her jaws widen
with the same ferocity.

Her teeth tear
with the same velocity.

In lieu of hiding
in leafy, green limbs,

she waits beneath the ice
like a spy
to give Penguin

      the surprise of its life.

Leopard seals are second only to orcas, or killer whales, as the continent's top predator. With powerful jaws, long teeth, and sinister eyes, their appearance matches their fierce reputation. Summer finds them prowling along the edges of Antarctic ice waiting for penguins to leave the rookery and plunge into the water. They have been known to consume as many as a dozen penguins a day. Leopard seals live solitary lives and only join with others of their kind during mating season.

Iceberg's farewell to Summer

Farewell, sun.
Thank you for highlighting
our bold stripes and brilliant hues.

Welcome, west wind.
We take comfort
in your unceasing song.

Farewell, Adélie penguins.
May pack ice provide safe passage
to warmer waves.

Welcome, thickening sea ice.
Won't you throw your cloak
across our shoulders?

Farewell, humpbacks and petrels.
Godspeed as you fly
through deep sky and ocean.

Welcome, darkness.
Shepherd us to sleep
as we await the sun's return.

Icebergs are huge chunks of freshwater ice that float in the cold, salty ocean waters. Only the tops of these ice mountains are visible, as 80 to 90 percent of the iceberg hides below the water's surface. As the sun sets—marking the season's end—the icebergs' vivid blue, green, and white coloration fades until they all but disappear in the darkness. Meanwhile, colder temperatures cause new ice to form, increasing the surface area of Antarctica to about twice its summer size. Migratory whales and penguins set off in search of warmer waters. Year-round residents like Weddell seals and emperor penguins limit their activity and take refuge in huddles or under the ice. Thanks to summer's bounty, these animals are prepared to survive Antarctica's harsh winter.

31

GLOSSARY

adept: highly skilled or well-trained

algae: any plants or plantlike organisms (like seaweed) that grow mostly in water

baleen whale: a type of whale that has baleen, or two rows of elastic plates used for filtering in and eating small ocean animals, instead of teeth

barnacles: small saltwater animals with feathery outgrowths for gathering food. They swim freely as larvae but as adults become permanently fastened to hard surfaces, such as rocks and the bottoms of ships.

bray: to produce a sound like the call of a donkey

brinicle: frozen salt water, or brine, at the bottom of the Southern Ocean. A barnacle is formed when salt water drips from melting sea ice and sinks rapidly into Antarctic waters.

créches: large groups of young (juvenile) penguins

dregs: solid matter, or sediment, that sinks to the bottom of a liquid

entombing: enclosing something as though it is in a tomb

fledge: to leave the nest or rookery after developing the feathers necessary for flying

flora: all the plants and plant life that live in a particular area or environment

glutton: someone who eats too much

hair grass: grass with slender, wiry stems or leaves. It grows in cool environments.

larva: an insect after it hatches from an egg and before it changes into its adult form. In this stage, the insect does not have wings. The plural is larvae.

molt: to shed, or cast off, skin, feathers, or fur and grow a new covering

mottled: marked with spots or blotches of different colors or shades of colors

nestlings: young birds that are not yet able to fly away from the nest

opaque: not letting light pass through; not transparent

piebald: having black and white spots or patches

predator: an animal that hunts and eats other animals

prey: an animal hunted by another animal for food

proboscis: a long, flexible snout

rookery: the place where a group of birds or social mammals (such as penguins or seals) breed, nest, or raise their young

silverfish: a species of fish that are important to the diet of Adélie penguins, whales, and Weddell seals. Silverfish produce antifreeze proteins that allow them to survive in the cold Antarctic waters.

FURTHER READING

Books

Amstutz, Lisa J. *Show Me Polar Animals.* Mankato, MN: Capstone, 2013.
Find out about the animals that inhabit the coldest parts of Earth—the Artic and Antarctic—and how these animals adapt to and survive cold climates.

Berger, Melvin, and Gilda Berger. *Penguins Swim but Don't Get Wet: And Other Amazing Facts about Polar Animals.* New York: Scholastic, 2004.
Did you know that emperor penguins will sometimes care for stones they mistake as eggs or that some penguins keel over in surprise when they see humans for the first time? This book offers these and other fun facts about polar animals.

Desmond, Jenni. *The Blue Whale.* New York: Enchanted Lion, 2015.
Take a closer look at the world's largest animal in this imaginatively illustrated book.

Hynes, Margaret. *Polar Lands.* Boston: Kingfisher, 2005.
This book will introduce you to animals that live in both the North and South Poles. You'll also learn more about the Arctic and Antarctic environments and the people who live in the North and South Poles. Explore the fun activities offered as well, like making your own iceberg and your own paper penguin mask.

Kalman, Bobbie, and Rebecca Sjonger. *Explore Antarctica.* St. Catherines, ONT: Crabtree, 2007.
Learn about Antarctica's animal and plant life, and explore the history of Antarctica from the earliest explorations to today.

Steele, Philip. *The Arctic and Antarctica.* New York: Kingfisher, 2013.
This book provides information on everything from the animals that occupy the North and South Poles to the history of Antarctic explorers and their expeditions.

Taylor, Barbara. *Arctic and Antarctic.* DK, 2012.
Take a tour through the Arctic and Antarctic and meet polar animals and polar people like the Inuit, Inupiat, and Yupik people.

Websites

"'Brinicle' Ice Finger of Death Filmed in Antarctic"
http://www.bbc.co.uk/nature/15835017
This time-lapse video shows a brinicle forming.

Discovering Antarctica
http://www.discoveringantarctica.org.uk/
This site offers activities, images, and video clips to help you learn about Antarctica in a fun and creative way.

National Geographic Crittercam
http://www.nationalgeographic.com/crittercam/antarctica/
Explore Antarctica through the eyes of a leopard seal and find out about other Antarctic animals through this interactive site.

National Geographic Discover Antarctica
http://ngm.nationalgeographic.com/ngm/antarctica/
This site offers an interactive map of Antarctica where you can explore different areas and even view videos of the Antarctic seas underneath the ice.

Scott Polar Research Institute
http://www.spri.cam.ac.uk/resources/kids/animals.html
The Scott Polar Research Institute website provides information about animals and birds that live in the Arctic and Antarctic.